The Alamo:
Flash Point Between Texas and Mexico

Edited by Mary Dodson Wade

Discovery Enterprises, Ltd.
Carlisle, Massachusetts

© Discovery Enterprises, Ltd., Carlisle, MA: 1996

ISBN 1-878668-95-1 paperback edition
Library of Congress Catalog Card Number 96-86709

10   9   8   7   6   5   4   3   2   1

Printed in the United States of America

Subject Reference Guide:

The Alamo: Flash Point Between Texas and Mexico
edited by Mary Dodson Wade
Texas History
The Alamo

Photos/Illustrations:

Front cover: Detail from *Fall of the Alamo — Death of Crockett*, (March 6, 1836). Engraving in *Davy Crockett's 1837 Almanack of Wild Sports in the West, Life in the Backwoods & Sketches of Texas*. From the Almanac Collection of the Rare Book and Special Collections Division of the Library of Congress.

Other illustrations: Credited where they appear in the book.

Table of Contents

Rivers

A Rio Grande
B Nueces
C San Antonio
D Colorado
E Brazos
F Trinity
G Sabine

Places

1 San Antonio de Béxar
2 The Alamo
3 Goliad
4 Gonzales
5 San Felipe de Austin
6 Washington-on-the Brazos
7 Anahuac
8 San Jacinto
9 Nacogdoches

Texas, outlined in the shape which eventually emerged

Introduction

by
Mary Dodson Wade

A small building in downtown San Antonio, Texas, stands as a symbol of courage in the face of overwhelming odds. Old and dilapidated in 1836, the chapel was an unlikely place to become a shrine. Standing just across the river from the sleepy outpost of San Antonio de Béxar, it had been the focal point of mission San Antonio de Valero. The mission had once been a sanctuary for descendants of the Canary Islanders who immigrated there in 1731. In time, it was converted from a religious to a military outpost and came to be known as the Alamo, Spanish for "cottonwood." More than a century and a half ago, dramatic events within and around the Alamo's walls became the ralling cry for a conflict that forever changed relations between Mexico and Texas.

For some three hundred years Spain had controlled the vast prairies, canyons, and pine forests that sweep across Texas. During the seventeenth and eighteenth centuries, although it jealously guarded its provinces in the Western Hemisphere against encroachment by France and England, Spain largely ignored the area. There was no gold or silver to ignite settlement fever.

Texas, nevertheless, had been the site of several attempts to establish missions to convert the native population. These had not been successful, and the outlying ones had withdrawn to the area around San Antonio. In 1820 there were only two real towns in Texas. Situated somewhat centrally, San Antonio de Béxar (or Béjar), which had been established in 1718, contained governmental offices. Ninety miles to the southeast lay La Bahía, also known as Goliad. In addition, Nacogdoches, site of a long-abandoned mission in east Texas, boasted a few scattered inhabitants.

Before the Alamo was a fortress, it was a mission named San Antonio de Valero. (Library of Congress)

Into this vacuum a restless entrepreneur named Moses Austin proposed to bring settlers from the United States. Austin, who had obtained Spanish citizenship at the time he moved into Missouri prior to the Louisiana Purchase, had lost his fortune in the bank collapse of 1819. He saw Spanish Texas as an opportunity to regain it and made a trip to San Antonio to confer with officials.

Early in 1821, after Austin's return to Missouri, Spain officially granted him permission to settle three hundred families. Under an *empresario* system he would act as administrator for the colony and receive land he could sell. While preparing to move his family, however, Austin died. His last request was for his son to undertake the enterprise.

Twenty-seven-year-old Stephen Fuller Austin had been living in New Orleans. He learned of his father's death when he arrived at their rendezvous and immediately assumed responsibility for the project. He went to San Antonio and worked out arrangements.

Almost immediately afterwards, Mexico threw off Spanish rule, and the younger Austin spent the next decade dealing with frequently changing governments. Through it all, he patiently carried out his duties. In order to assure colonists clear title to their land, he spent over a year in Mexico City negotiating with one government after another. He considered himself a Mexican citizen and learned Spanish in order to explain the laws. He signed documents as "Estévan F. Austin." There were other *empresarios*, but none more successful because he personally administered his grants.

Lured by land that was almost free, people from the United States poured in. "G.T.T." signs on abandoned property in the East let the world know that the former residents had "Gone to Texas." Beyond good citizenship and a nominal membership in the Catholic Church, little was required of them. They were even exempt from taxes for several years. Within ten years, twenty thousand Anglos lived in Texas.

Inevitably, conflicts arose. Settlers did not think of themselves as Mexicans and spoke little Spanish. They resented laws that did not guarantee the personal freedoms they were accustomed to find in the United States. Not even significant changes enacted with the Constitution of 1824 granted everything they wanted.

One point of contention was the fact that Texas was part of the state of Coahuila y Tejas (Texas). The state's capital was hundreds of miles away. There was provision for Texas to attain statehood when it had sufficient population, but the influx of American settlers propelled events in quite the opposite direction. The Mexican government, which at first welcomed settlers as a buffer against the Indians, became alarmed. In 1830, fearing that the United States intended to annex Texas, it closed the borders to immigration.

Texans — Texians, as they referred to themselves — met to vent their feelings. At the consultation of 1832, they petitioned for statehood. Mexican officials were in no mood to grant it.

A second convention the following year formally drafted the statehood proposal, and Austin was sent to Mexico City with the request. He managed to get the borders opened to immigrants but was unable to gain separate statehood. After writing a letter to the council in San Antonio urging them to organize anyway, he started home. Some officials who read the letter viewed it as sedition. The Mexican government intercepted Austin and returned him to Mexico City as a prisoner.

During his two-year detainment, part of which was spent in solitary confinement, the quiet, educated man who had advocated working within the laws of Mexico realized things were not going to change. When he returned to Texas, he called for Texans to decide on a course of action. The Texans knew what they wanted. In the fall of 1835, delegates at San Felipe de Austin, while acknowledging Mexico's constitutionally elected government, made it plain that they would resist the armies of dictator Antonio López de Santa Anna.

During Austin's absence Texans had already skirmished with the Mexican military. In June 1835, three months before his return, the Mexican garrison at Anahuac at the head of Galveston Bay had come under attack from a rambunctious militia outfit led by William Barret Travis. In response, General Martín Perfecto de Cós, Santa Anna's brother-in-law and military commander of the northern provinces, boasted that his soldiers would silence the settlers. He led five hundred trained solders to San Antonio to carry out his orders.

Once there, Cós sent a detachment of soldiers to demand the return of a cannon that had been given to the people of Gonzales for protection from the Indians. Rather than complying, the towns-people adopted a "come-and-take-it" attitude and turned the cannon on the soldiers. The Mexicans quickly retreated to San Antonio.

Less than a week later, in another victorious skirmish, Texans captured Goliad. Then, the "Army of the People" marched from Gonzales to San Antonio. Determined to drive Cós out, they put the town under siege.

Because of his past leadership, Austin was elected commander of the voluntary troops at San Antonio, but delegates gathered at San Felipe needed his skills as a diplomat. In late November, Colonel Edward Burleson replaced Austin as commander of the troops, and he went to the United States to raise recruits and money. As a result, the Father of Texas was not in Texas during the critical days of early 1836.

By December, the Texans holding the siege became discouraged. Not even the arrival of the New Orleans Greys helped their outlook. Suddenly there was a reversal as men responded to the call, "Who will go with old Ben Milam?" Milam, who had recently joined them after escaping from Mexican captors, led the assault. He and another man lost their lives, but Cós surrendered. Given safe passage in exchange for a promise not to return, the Mexican general withdrew his troops to Mexico.

Wild rejoicing erupted when Cós left. The Texans assumed they had won and that their demands would be met. With winter at hand, they believed that no response could come from Mexico City, at least not until the following spring. They reckoned without the fury of the Mexican dictator. Stung by Cós's defeat, he moved swiftly.

Santa Anna, born in 1794 in Jalapa, capital of the province of Veracruz, had risen to the highest office in the land as the result of a distinguished military career. He had taken office during a troubled period when there were deep divisions in political ideology. The Centralists supported a strong government with power concentrated in the country's leader. The Federalists wanted the states to have more say in government decisions.

Santa Anna first posed as a Federalist, supporting the constitution with its representative form of government. He won election to the presidency in 1833 on a liberal platform. Once in office, however, the forty-year-old president reversed himself. Within a year, he stamped out all opposition and ruled as a dictator.

In Santa Anna's quest to consolidate control, Texas loomed as a particularly vulnerable region. He believed, as many Mexicans did, that the United States was planning to grab it. Cós's defeat reinforced that fear, and Santa Anna vowed to drive all Americans back across the Sabine River.

Based upon its history, his army appeared capable of backing up

9

the threat. It was well organized, with veteran officers in command of troops that were well trained and equipped. Having recently crushed a rebellion in Zacatecas, Santa Anna rode at the head of the army gathered to force Texas into submission.

Neither troops nor circumstances were the same for this new venture, however. While there were veteran battalions, including Cós's returning troops, whom Santa Anna ordered to join the campaign, this army also included convicts and raw recruits. All were force-marched northward across desolate terrain, suffering intensely from freak winter snow storms in uniforms intended for a warmer climate. The long distances, with little population from which to secure food, resulted in inadequate supplies.

In spite of the difficult conditions, Mexican troops reached San Antonio in February 1836, and startled Texans retreated across the river to the Alamo. The Texans numbered about 150 because many of those involved in the siege had marched south to carry the fight into Mexico and were soon captured.

The Alamo, a rectangular enclosure of some three acres, included several buildings besides the chapel. It was not built as a fortress, but Cós had strengthened it before his retreat. Two strong commanders were now in charge. Regular soldiers served under dashing Colonel William Barret Travis, while the rowdy volunteers answered to Colonel James Bowie.

The defenders were a diverse group. The men from Texas included colonists as well as *Tejanos* (Hispanic Texans). The Americans came from many states. David Crockett with his Tennessee volunteers had arrived just two weeks earlier. Men born in England, Scotland, and Wales were there. Germans had come with the New Orleans Greys. Also within the walls were several families with children.

On February 23, 1836, Santa Anna reached San Antonio, ran up a red flag of "no quarter," and demanded surrender. Travis answered with a cannon shot, and the thirteen-day siege began.

Oddly enough, the Texans had little trouble slipping through the lines. Travis sent couriers with eloquent pleas for reinforcement, and thirty-two men from Gonzales made their way into the Alamo on March 1. James Butler Bonham made it to Goliad and learned that Colonel James Fannin was not coming with his force of five hundred men. Declaring that Travis deserved an answer, Bonham turned his horse toward San Antonio and rode to his death. Juan Sequín, another courier, joined Sam Houston at Gonzales. He lived to lead a group of *Tejanos* fighting against the Mexicans at San Jacinto.

Those in the Alamo probably never knew that delegates meeting at Washington-on-the-Brazos had signed the Texas Declaration of Independence on March 2. Sam Houston placed his signature on the document on his forty-third birthday. Several days later he set out for San Antonio. It was too late.

As dawn broke on March 6, the Alamo presented a grisly scene. In three successive assaults Mexican soldiers had breached the north wall, climbing over the bodies of their comrades. Estimates of the number used in the attack vary widely. One respected scholar, Walter Lord, believed it was not more than eighteen hundred, though four thousand is a figure that has also been put forward. For total Mexican casualties, Lord accepted six hundred and for Mexicans killed, two hundred. Under orders from Santa Anna, no defenders survived. Lord estimated that 183 died while the roster presented below, on pages 61 and 62, lists 189. Only women, children, and some slaves were spared. Susanna Dickinson, her husband among those killed, was sent to tell the world the fate that awaited rebellious settlers.

In effect, Santa Anna had given the Texans a battle cry: "Remember the Alamo!"

The Rising Conflict

*When Stephen Austin returned from Mexico in September 1835,
he called for an assembly to determine what action Texas should take.
Delegates in hot debate finally acknowledged the Constitution of 1824 but
set up a provisional government and declared themselves free of Santa
Anna's regime.*

Source: "Declaration of the People of Texas in General Convention Assembled," *Journals
of the Consultation Held at San Felipe de Austin, October 16, 1835* (Published by Order
of Congress, Houston, 1838), pp. 21-2, quoted in Ernest Wallace, David M. Vigness,
and George B. Ward, editors, *Documents of Texas History*, 2d edition (Austin: State
House Press, 1994), p. 91.

Whereas, General Antonio Lopez de Santa Anna and other Military
Chieftains have, by force of arms, overthrown the Federal Institutions
of Mexico, and dissolved the Social Compact which existed between
Texas and the other Members of the Mexican Confederacy—Now,
the good People of Texas, availing themselves of their natural rights,

SOLEMNLY DECLARE

1st. That they have taken up arms in defence of their rights and
Liberties, which were threatened by the encroachments of military
despots, and in defence of the Republican Principles of the Federal
Constitution of Mexico of eighteen hundred and twenty-four.

2d. That Texas is no longer, morally or civilly, bound by the
compact of Union; yet, stimulated by the generosity and sympathy
common to a free people they offer their support and assistance to
such Mexicans of the Mexican Confederacy as will take up arms
against their military despotism.

3d. That they do not acknowledge, that the present authorities of
the nominal Mexican Republic have the right to govern within the
limits of Texas.

4th. That they will not cease to carry on war against the said authorities, whilst their troops are within the limits of Texas.

5th. That they hold it to be their right, during the disorganization of the Federal System and the reign of despotism, to withdraw from the Union, to establish an independent Government, or to adopt such measures as they may deem best calculated to protect their rights and liberties; but that they will continue faithful to the Mexican Government so long as that nation is governed by the Constitution and Laws that were formed for the government of the Political Association.

6th. That Texas is responsible for the expenses of her Armies now in the field.

7th. That the public faith is pledged for the payment of any debts contracted by her Agents.

8th. That she will reward by donations in Land, all who volunteer their services in her present struggle, and receive them as Citizens.

These *Declarations* we solemnly avow to the world, and call GOD to witness their truth and sincerity; and invoke defeat and disgrace upon our heads should we prove guilty of duplicity.

[P. B. Dexter], *Secretary*   B. T. Archer, *President*

In December 1835, Texans held Mexican forces in San Antonio under siege, but there was dissension about continuing the action. Ben Milam rallied the Texans but lost his life during the assault. Colonel Frank Johnson, who assumed command, gave this third-person account.

Source: Frank W. Johnson, *A History of Texas and Texans*, edited and brought to date by Eugene C. Barker with the assistance of Ernest William Winkler, vol. I (New York: The American Historical Society, 1916), pp. 351-9.

The question of raising the siege, and going into winter quarters, either at Goliad or Gonzales, or at both places, was being discussed at headquarters in the first days of December....This action, though approved by a majority of the officers and men composing the army, was regarded by others as fatal to the campaign, and would result in breaking up the volunteer force, which was then the last hope of Texas....

[T]he Quartermaster was directed to have the trains loaded and ready to move with the army on the 5th. About the middle of the afternoon [the 4th],...a Lieutenant of the Mexican army, a deserter, entered our camp....He reported the defences of the town weak....After hearing his report, Colonel Johnson suggested to Colonel Milam to call for volunteers, that "now is the time." Most of the army had gathered at the headquarters of General Burleson. Milam called in a clear, loud voice "who will go with Old Ben Milam into San Antonio?" Many answered "I will," whereupon they were requested to fall into line....[W]e had but three hundred and one men....

The first division was to enter the town by the first street running north from the public square, and occupy the De la Garza house, within musket range of the square; the second division was to march near the river and take possession of the Veramendi house.

Thus organized...the twin divisions took up the line of march just before day on the morning of the 5th of December. Erastus or Deaf Smith and Norwich were guides of the second division, and H. Arnold and John W. Smith, guides of the first division....

[W]e collected all the mining tools we had — one shovel, two crow-bars, and one pick — and having prepared sandbags during the day, made details of men to open a communication between the two divisions....General Burleson visited the second division at night of the first day, and brought with him the first beef that we had had since leaving camp. Colonel Johnson crossed over to the first division and reported success and casualties to Colonel Milam. The troops of both divisions were not only cheerful but enthusiastic....

[The second day.] Having got our artillery under cover, we opened a well directed fire on the town....

On the morning of the third day, at daylight, it was discovered that the enemy had thrown up an embankment on the Alamo side of the river...from which they opened a brisk fire of small arms, which was seconded by the guns of the Alamo; however, they were soon silenced by our rifles and driven from their position....

Benjamin R. Milam, whose name will and ought ever to be held in grateful and honored remembrance by Texans, was born of humble parents in the state of Kentucky, and received but an imperfect education. He was six feet high, of fine form and commanding appearance....[F]ortified by habits of independence, he associated with the Indian tribes, in order to explore the more southerly portions of Texas. In the war with Great Britain, in 1812-15, he acquired a high reputation among his countrymen; but...at the close of the war, he engaged in the struggle then going on in Mexico for independence, and soon distinguished himself by his courage, zeal, and love of freedom....Escaping from Monterey, where he had been imprisoned with Governor Viesea and others, in 1835, he made his way to Texas. He had crossed the San Antonio river near Goliad. Faint and tired, he took shelter in a bunch of bushes. The approach of Captain Collinsworth's company attracted his attention. Naturally supposing them to be a squad of Mexican soldiers, he determined to defend himself to the death. To his astonishment and joy, the advancing force proved to be his fellow-colonists of Texas, who were marching against Goliad. He, at once, decided to join the volunteers as a private, although accustomed and well qualified to command. He was among the foremost in the assault. He remained a few days after the capture of the fort, and then joined the army of General Austin near San Antonio.

When [Milam was] killed, the Masonic fraternity, then present, took charge of his body, and, with a proper detail of troops, he was buried in the yard — east side — of the Veramendi house, with military honors. His remains were subsequently disinterred and deposited in the old burying ground west of the town, with appropriate Masonic and military honor.

At a meeting of the officers of both divisions, at 7 o'clock P. M., Colonel F. W. Johnson was unanimously chosen commander of the assaulting force.

The fourth day was wet and cold, with but little firing on either side. Early in the day, the companies holding the Navarro house, aided by the Grays, advanced and took position on the Zambrano Row, which led to the Military Square. Our brave boys fought their way from house to house....

Immediately after daylight [fifth day] it was discovered that the enemy had hauled down his flag, and hoisted in its stead a white flag. Soon after a bearer of a flag of truce was brought to the headquarters of Colonel Johnson, and declared the desire of General Cos to capitulate....

Herewith is subjoined the report of General Burleson:

"BEXAR, December 14th, 1835.

"To His Excellency Henry Smith, Provisional Governor of Texas:

"SIR: I have the satisfaction to enclose a copy of Colonel Johnson's account of the storming and surrender of San Antonio de Bexar, to which I have little to add that can in any way increase the luster of this brilliant achievement...which will, I trust, prove the downfall of the last position of military despotism on our soil of freedom....

"On the morning of the 9th, in consequence of advice from Col. Johnson of a flag of truce having been sent in, to intimate a desire to capitulate, I proceeded to town, and by two o'clock a. m. of the 10th, a treaty was finally concluded...deeming the terms highly favorable, considering the strong position and large force of the enemy, which could not be less than thirteen hundred effective men....

"General Cos left this morning for the mission of San José, and, tomorrow, commences his march to the Rio Grande, after complying with all that had been stipulated....

"Tomorrow I leave the garrison and town under command of Colonel Johnson, with sufficient number of men and officers to sustain the same, in case of attack, until assisted from the colonies; so that your Excellency may consider our conquest as sufficiently secured against every attempt of the enemy. The rest of the army will retire to their homes.

"I have the honor to be, Your Excellency's obedient servant,

"Edward Burleson
"Commander in Chief of the Volunteer Army."

Help for Texas

Calls to aid Texas reached the United States, and volunteers came from many states. However Texas needed money, and in December 1835, Stephen F. Austin, with two other envoys, went to the United States to seek loans. Their tour took them up the Mississippi and Ohio Rivers on their way to Washington, D.C. While in Louisville, Kentucky, Austin spoke at a meeting arranged by his cousin, Mary Austin Holley. In this classic speech he recounted Texas history, justifying Texas's actions. Many Kentucky volunteers responded, although most arrived too late to participate in the revolution.

Source: Stephen Fuller Austin, speech, Second Presbyterian Church, Louisville, Kentucky, March 5, 1836, quoted in Louis J. Wortham, *A History of Texas: From Wilderness to Commonwealth*, vol. 3 (Fort Worth: Wortham-Molyneaux Company, 1924), pp. 146-70.

It is with the most unfeigned and heartfelt gratitude that I appear before this enlightened audience to thank the citizens of Louisville, as I do in the name of the people of Texas, for the kind and generous sympathy they have manifested in favor of the cause of that struggling country, and to make a plain statement of facts explanatory of the contest in which Texas is engaged with the Mexican government.

The public has been informed through the medium of the newspapers that war existed between the people of Texas and the present government of Mexico. There are, however, many circumstances connected with this contest, its origin, its principles, and objects, which, perhaps, are not so generally known, and are indispensable to a full and proper elucidation of this subject.

When a people consider themselves compelled by circumstances or by oppression to appeal to arms and resort to their natural rights, they necessarily submit their cause to the great tribunal of public opinion. The people of Texas, confident of the justice of their cause, fearlessly and cheerfully appeal to this tribunal. In doing this, the first step is to show, as I trust I shall be able to do by succinct statement of facts, that our cause is just, and is the cause of right and liberty; the same holy cause for which our forefathers fought and bled; the same that has an advocate in the bosom of every freeman, no matter in what country or by what people it may be contended for.

But a few years back Texas was a wilderness, the home of the uncivilized Comanches and other tribes of Indians, who waged a constant and ruinous warfare against the Spanish settlements. These settlements at that time were limited to the small towns of Béxar (commonly called San Antonio) and Goliad, situated on the western limits. The incursions of the Indians ended beyond the Rio Bravo del Norte [Rio Grande] and desolated that part of the country.

In order to restrain these savages and bring them into subjection, the government opened Texas for settlement. Foreign emigrants were invited and called to that country. American enterprise accepted that invitation and promptly responded to the call. The first colony of Americans or foreigners ever settled in Texas was by myself. It was commenced in 1821 under a permission to my father, Moses Austin, from the Spanish government, previous to the independence of Mexico, and has succeeded by surmounting those difficulties and dangers incident to all new and wilderness countries infested by hostile Indians. These difficulties were many and at times appalling, and can only be appreciated by the hardy pioneers of this western country, who have passed through similar scenes.

The question here naturally occurs: What inducements, what prospects, what hopes could have stimulated us, the pioneers and settlers of Texas, to remove from the midst of civilized society, to expatriate ourselves from this land of liberty; from this our native country, endeared to us as it was, and still is and ever will be, by the ties of nativity, the reminiscences of childhood and youth and local attachments, of friendship and relationship? Can it for a moment be supposed that we severed all these ties — the ties of nature and of education — and went to Texas to grapple with the wilderness and savage foes merely from a spirit of wild and visionary adventure, without guarantees of protection for our persons and property and political rights? No! It cannot be believed. No American, no Englishman, no one of any nation who has a knowledge of the people of the United States or of the prominent characteristics of the Anglo-Saxon race to which we belong — a race that in all ages and in all countries wherever it has appeared has been marked by a jealous and tenacious watchfulness of its liberties, and for a cautious and calculating view of the probable events of the future no one who has a knowledge of this race can or will believe that we moved to Texas without such guarantees as free-born and enterprising men naturally expect and require.

The fact is, we had such guarantees; for, in the first place, the government bound itself to protect us by the mere act of admitting us as citizens, on the general and long-established principle, even in the dark ages, that protection and allegiance are reciprocal — a principle which in this enlightened age has been extended much further; for its revised interpretation now is, that the object of government is the well-being, security, and happiness of the governed, and that allegiance ceases whenever it is clear, evident and palpable that this object is in no respect effected....

To conclude, I have shown that our cause is just and righteous, that it is the great cause of mankind, and as such merits the approbation and moral support of this magnanimous and free people, that our object is independence as a new republic, or to become a State of the United States; that our resources are sufficient to sustain the principles we are defending; that the results will be the promotion of the great cause of liberty, of philanthropy and religion, and of the protection of a great and important interest of the people of the United States.

With these claims to the approbation and moral support of the free of all nations, the people of Texas have taken up arms in self-defense, and they submit their cause to the judgment of an impartial world and to the protection of a just and omnipotent God.

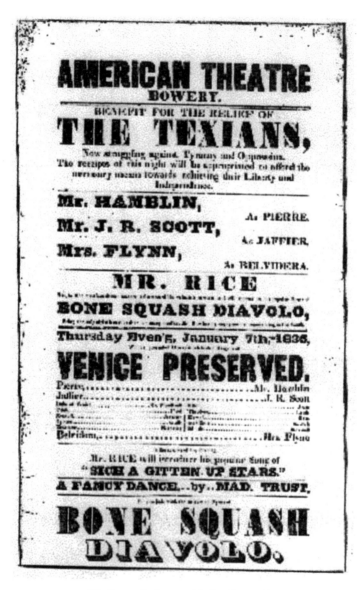

AMERICAN THEATRE
BOWERY.
BENEFIT FOR THE RELIEF OF

THE TEXANS,

Now struggling against Tyranny and Oppression.
The receipts of this night will be appropriated to afford the
necessary means towards achieving their Liberty and
Independence.

Mr. HAMBLIN,
As PIERRE.

Mr. J. R. SCOTT,
As JAFFIER.

Mrs. FLYNN,
As BELVIDERA.

MR. RICE

BONE SQUASH DIAVOLO,

Thursday Even'g, January 7th, 1836,

VENICE PRESERVED.

Pierre..Mr. Hamblin
Jaffier..J. R. Scott
Belvidera,..................................Mrs. Flynn

Mr. RICE will introduce his popular Song of
"SICH A GITTEN UP STARS."
A FANCY DANCE...by...MAD. TRUST.

BONE SQUASH
DIAVOLO.

The Texans had support in far distant places.
(Library of Congress)

Herman Ehrenberg, an educated, German-born eighteen-year-old, was among the volunteers who formed the New Orleans Greys to help Texas fight for independence. The lighthearted Greys reached San Antonio, met a Texas legend, and helped defeat Cós. Several months later, when Mexican troops massacred Colonel James Fannin's forces near Goliad, Ehrenberg was among the small number who escaped by swimming away.

Source: Herman Ehrenberg, *With Milam and Fannin: Adventures of a German Boy in Texas' Revolution*, translated by Charlotte Churchill, edited by Henry Smith (Dallas: Tardy Publishing Company, Inc., 1935), pp. 1-153.

At every corner of the evenly laid-out streets of New Orleans, placards two feet high called the citizens' attention to a mass meeting which would be held in the Arcade at eight o'clock that evening. The gathering, sponsored by the Committee for Texas, had been arranged to help the prairie country in its struggle against Santa Anna's tyranny. Reminding the people of New Orleans that the men who asked their assistance were Americans, the Committee appealed to the patriotism of the community and urged everyone to attend the meeting organized for the relief of these countrymen in distress.

Reports of the events in Texas filled the newspapers of the city....The success of this propaganda was complete, for all the citizens of New Orleans...were ready to help the brave men who were fighting against Mexican oppression.

The following afternoon, October 12, 1835, I went aboard the *Washita* with the first party of volunteers who left for Texas. We formed the first company of Greys....Although we went aboard shortly after we had enlisted, we had had time to provide ourselves with ready-made clothes suitable to prairie life. The greyish color of these garments, which we had found in the warehouses of the city, accounts for the name of our company. The weapons of each man consisted of a rifle, pistols, and the bowie-knife....

When we got to [Texas],...a pretty Texas girl held out to us a beautiful banner of blue silk, bearing the following inscription: "To the

21

first company of volunteers sent by New Orleans to Texas." [*Editor's note. Santa Anna sent this banner from the Alamo to Mexico City.*]

After we had kissed the soil of our new country and become its citizens, we continued our march....[T]he militia came to meet us to the accompaniment of the muffled tones of a drum from which the drummer...drew most melancholy sounds...not at all in unison with the mood of the enthusiastic Greys. Our drummer, therefore, began to roll out the lively march of "Beer in the Mug."...

One of the main diversions we had in our camp on the San Antonio river was to go through the cornfield lying between us and the city to a small redoubt....

Inside the redoubt, we found our friends busy with the loading, pointing, and firing of the guns....

"A hundred neat and handy musket balls against twenty," shouted one, "that I hit the old barracks between the third and fourth windows."

"Done," answered two or three voices at once. The gunner fired — and then had to spend the whole of the next day casting bullets.

"My pistols — by the way, the best in the place," yelled another contestant, who likewise was going to fire the gun, "against the worst ones in the camp."

"Well, sir, I reckon I can risk it," said a pioneer wrapped in a green frieze-coat....Away flew the shot, and the forfeited pistols of the pointer now adorned the belt of the man in the frieze-coat, who magnanimously took his own and handed them to the loser, as he said: "Look here, friend, I will also fire the gun once. If I miss my aim, then I'll return your pistols."

Immediately after saying these words, this new competitor in our shooting match loaded the gun and brought it to the proper elevation. He went about his task more slowly than those who had tried before him....Screwing up one eye, he carefully examined his objective, ascertained its probable distance, and for a while remained deeply absorbed in his mathematical computations. As he was deaf, the noisy bustle in the redoubt left him undisturbed....Finally, after he had spent some time adjusting his aim, he lit the fuse....[W]hen the vapors which darkened the atmosphere had blown off, the Greys and their comrades looked in vain for the third and fourth windows of the fortress. Unanimous applause greeted this feat of old Deaf Smith, as he was called. A little later on we found that this proficient gunner was also the boldest and most expert hunter on the Texas prairie....

Erastus "Deaf" Smith (Library of Congress)

When the Greys heard the good news [the decision to storm San Antonio], they romped and yelled with joy....

...One of our best artillerymen, an Englishman named Cook, was killed during the third day of our siege. This was a serious blow for us, for having served in the British fleet, Cook was an experienced hand and we greatly missed the skill of this well-trained marine. He was the first man to die while on duty at the twelve-pounder.

The death of our valiant Colonel Milam on the same day was another and greater tragedy. He was struck in the head by a bullet...and died instantly. We buried the two bodies quietly at night. Their funeral march was the loud, monotonous boom of the enemy's cannon, while the black and idle muzzles of our silent artillery were the only tokens of grief and esteem we could give to the two brave men who had died in action....

Shortly after the enemy's departure [Cós's troops] most of my comrades and I set up our living quarters in the ruins of the Alamo....Although traces of its architectural ornaments were still extant, it looked small and plain compared with the large city church. Tall arches adorned the main entrance of the Alamo chapel, but as they had reached a dangerous stage of disintegration, no one dared tarry long under their fragile curves. Statues of saints carved in sandstone decorated the outer walls, and every morning Mexican women would stop to pray in front of these holy images....

The restoration of peace had brought back to the city many of its residents who had deserted it during the siege....

Mexicans are great pleasure-seekers, and spend their lives in dancing, riding, eating, drinking, and sleeping. As we were welcome guests among many of the native families in the city, we visited them often.

The Alamo under Siege

Outnumbered and under siege at the Alamo, Travis sent a number of appeals for aid, but the only help that arrived was a thirty-two-man contingent from Gonzales that entered the Alamo on March 1. Travis's letter has become a classic.

Source: William Barret Travis, letter, February 24, 1836, quoted in *The Papers of the Texas Revolution, 1835-1836*, edited by John H. Jenkins, vol. 4 (Austin: Presidial Press, 1973), p. 423.

To the People of Texas & All Americans in the World — Fellow Citizens & Compatriots — I am besieged by a thousand or more of the Mexicans under Santa Anna. I have sustained a continual Bombardment & cannonade for 24 hours and have not lost a man. The enemy has demanded a surrender at discretion, otherwise, the garrison are to be put to the sword, if the fort is taken. I have answered the demand with a cannon shot, & our flag still waves proudly from the walls. *I shall never surrender or retreat.* Then, I call on you in the name of Liberty, of patriotism & everything dear to the American character, to come to our aid with all dispatch. The enemy is receiving reinforcements daily & will no doubt increase to three or four thousand in four or five days. If this call is neglected, I am determined to sustain myself as long as possible & die like a soldier who never forgets what is due his own honor and that of his country. VICTORY OR DEATH.

> William Barret Travis
> Lt. Col. comdt.

P.S. - The Lord is on our side. When the enemy appeared in sight we had not three bushels of corn. We have since found in deserted houses 80 to 90 bushels and got into the walls 20 or 30 head of Beeves.

Sequín, a fifth-generation resident of San Antonio, sided with the Texans. Sent from the Alamo on February 28, 1836, to seek aid, he met Francis Desauque, who had foraged Sequín's ranch. Desauque returned to Goliad and died in the massacre. Sequín joined Houston at Gonzales and fought at San Jacinto. Branded a traitor for his involvement in a Mexican raid on San Antonio in 1842, Sequín subsequently returned from Mexico and published his memoirs of the Texas Revolution to clear his name.

Source: Jesús F. de la Teja, editor, *A Revolution Remembered: The Memoirs and Selected Correspondence of Juan N. Sequín* (Austin: State House Press, 1991), pp. 107-8.

On the 22nd of February at two o'clock P.M., General Santa Anna took possession of the city [San Antonio] with over 4000 men and in the mean time we fell back on the Alamo.

On the 28th, the enemy commenced the bombardment, meanwhile we met in a Council of War, and taking into consideration our perilous situation, it was resolved by a majority of the council that I should leave the fort and proceed with a communication to Colonel Fannin, requesting him to come to our assistance. I left the Alamo on the night of the council; on the following day I met, at the Ranch of San Bartolo on the Cibolo, Captain Desac who, by orders of Fannin, had foraged on my ranch, carrying off a great number of beeves, corn, &c. Desac informed me that Fannin could not delay more than two days his arrival at the Cibolo, on his way to render assistance to the defenders of the Alamo. I therefore determined to wait for him. I sent Fannin, by express, the communication from Travis, informing him at the same time of the critical position of the defenders of the Alamo. Fannin answered me, through Lieutenant Finley, that he had advanced as far as "Rancho Nuevo" but, being informed of the movements of General Urrea, he had counter-marched to Goliad, to defend that place; adding that he could not respond to Travis' call, their respective commands being separate....

On the 6th of March, I received orders to go to San Antonio with my company and a party of American citizens, carrying on the horses provisions for the defenders of the Alamo.

Arrived at the Cibolo and, not hearing the signal gun which was to be discharged every fifteen minutes as long as the place held out, we retraced our steps to convey to the General-in-Chief the sad tidings. A new party was sent out, which soon came back, having met with Anselmo Vergara and Andres Barcena, both soldiers of my company, whom I had left for purposes of observation in the vicinity of San Antonio; they brought the intelligence of the fall of the Alamo. Their report was so circumstantial as to preclude any doubts about that disastrous event.

Louis Eyth. Legend of Travis drawing a line with his sword. (Daughters of the Republic of Texas Library. CN96.371)

Assault on the Alamo

Santa Anna's secret orders for the assault cover minute details along with commanders and columns that were to participate. Untrained recruits were to remain in their quarters.

Source: [Antonio López de Santa Anna], as conveyed by Juan Valentine Amador, General Orders, March 5, 1836, quoted in *The Papers of the Texas Revolution, 1835-1836*, edited by John H. Jenkins, vol. 4 (Austin: Presidial Press, 1973), pp. 518-9.

Army of Operations.
General Orders of the 5th of March, 1836.
2 o'clock P.M. — Secret

To the Generals, Chiefs of Sections, and Commanding Officers:

The time has come to strike a decisive blow upon the enemy occupying the Fortress of the Alamo. Consequently, His Excellency, the General in Chief, has decided that, tomorrow, at 4 o'clock A.M., the columns of attack shall be stationed at musket-shot distance from the first entrenchments, reach for the charge, which shall commence, at a signal given with the bugle, from the Northern Battery.

The first column will be commanded by General Don Martin Perfecto de Cos, and, in his absence, by myself.

The Permanent Battalion of Aldama (except the company of Grenadiers) and the three right centre companies of the Active Battalion of San Luis, will comprise the first column.

The second column will be commanded by Colonel Don Francisco Duque, and, in his absence, by General Don Manuel Fernandez Castrillon; it will be composed of the Active Battalion of Toluca (except the company of Grenadiers) and the three remaining centre companies of the Active Battalion of San Luis.

Antonio López de Santa Anna
(Library of Congress)

The third column will be commanded by Colonel Jose Maria Romero, and, in his absence, by Colonel Mariano Salas; it will be composed of the Permanent Battalion of Matamoros and Jimenes.

The fourth column will be commanded by Colonel Juan Morales, and, in his absence, by Colonel Jose Minon; it will be composed of the light companies of the Battalions of Matamoros and Jimenes, and of the Active Battalion of San Luis.

His Excellency, the General-in-chief, will, in due time, designate the points of attack, and give his instructions to the Commanding Officers.

The reserve will be composed of the Battalion of Engineers and the five companies of Grenadiers of the Permanent Battalions of Matamoros, Jimenes and Aldama, and the Active Battalion of Toluca and San Luis.

The reserve will be commanded by the General-in-chief in person, during the attack; but General Augustin Amat will assemble this party, which will report to him, this evening at 5 o'clock, to be marched to the designated station.

The first column will carry ten ladders, two crowbars and two axes; the second, ten ladders; the third, six ladders; and the fourth, two ladders.

The men calladers [men carrying ladders] will sling their guns on their shoulders, to be enabled to place the ladders wherever they may be required.

The companies of Grenadiers will be supplied with six packages of cartridges to every man, and the centre companies with two packages and two spare flints. The men will wear neither overcoats nor blankets, nor anything that may impede the rapidity of their motions. The Commanding Officers will see that the men have the chin straps of their caps down, and that they wear either shoes or sandals.

The troops composing the columns of attack will turn in to sleep at dark; to be in readiness to move at 12 o'clock at night.

Recruits deficient in instruction will remain in their quarters. The arms, principally the bayonets, should be in perfect order.

As soon as the moon rises, the centre companies of the Active Battalion of San Luis will abandon the points they are now occupying on the line, in order to have time to prepare.

The Cavalry, under Colonel Joaquin Ramirez y Sesma, will be stationed at the Alameda, saddling up at 3 o'clock A. M. It shall be its duty to scout the country, to prevent the possibility of an escape.

The honor of the nation being interested in this engagement against the bold and lawless foreigners who are opposing us, His Excellency expects that every man will do his duty, and exert himself to give a day of glory to the country, and of gratification to the Supreme Government, who will know how to reward the distinguished deeds of the brave soldiers of the Army of Operations.

> Juan Valentine Amador
> [for Santa Anna]

A certified copy:
Bexar, March 6th, 1836
Ramon Martinez Caro,
    Secretary.

Potter visited the Alamo battle site in 1860, made measurements, and produced a map. Using information gathered from participants he published this account of the battle but fails to mention one adult male survivor: Brigido Guerrero, a Mexican citizen who convinced his countrymen he had been held prisoner.

Source: R[uben] M. Potter, "The Fall of the Alamo," *Magazine of American History*, 2, no. 1 (January 1878), pp. 1-21.

...[The Alamo] was an old fabric, built during the first settlement of the vicinity by the Spaniards; and having been originally designed as a place of safety for the colonists and their property in case of Indian hostility, with room sufficient for that purpose, it had neither the strength, compactness, nor dominant points which ought to belong to a regular fortification. The front of the Alamo chapel bears date of 1757, but the other works must have been built earlier. As the whole area contained between two and three acres, a thousand men would have barely sufficed to man its defenses....

From recollection of the locality, as I viewed it in 1841, I could in 1860 trace the extent of the outer walls, which had been demolished about thirteen years before the latter period. The dimensions here given are taken from actual measurements then made....[C]hapel of the fort [was] seventy-five feet long, sixty-two wide, and twenty-two and one-half high, with walls of solid masonry, four feet thick. It was originally of but one story, and if it then had any windows below, they were probably walled up when the place was prepared for defense. [A] platform [was] in the east end of the chapel. [A] wall, fifty feet long and about 12 high, connect[ed] the chapel with the long barrack. The latter was a stone house of two stories, one hundred and eighty-six feet long, eighteen wide and eighteen high. [A] low, one-story stone barrack, one hundred and fourteen feet long and seventeen wide, [had] in the center a *porte-cochere*. The walls of these two houses were about thirty inches thick, and they had flat terrace roofs of beams and plank, covered with a thick coat of cement. [F]lat-roofed, stone-walled rooms [were] built against the inside of the west barrier....[B]arrier walls...[enclosed] an area, one hundred and fifty-four yards long, and fifty-four wide, with the long barrack on the east and the low barrack on the south of it. These walls were two and three-quarter feet thick, and from nine to twelve feet high, except the strip which fronted the chapel, that being only four feet in height. This low piece of wall was covered by an oblique entrenchment...which ran from the southwest angle of the chapel to the east end of the low barrack....[A] palisade gate [was] at the west end of the entrenchment....Several rooms...opened upon the large area. Most of those doors had within a semicircular parapet for the use of marksmen, composed of a double curtain of hides upheld by stakes and filled in with rammed earth. Some of the rooms were also loopholed....[B]arrier walls, from five to six feet high and

33

two and three-quarter feet thick...enclosed a smaller area north of the chapel and east of the long barrack....[A] cattle yard east of the barrack and south of the small area...was enclosed by a picket fence....[A] battered breach [was] in the north wall.

The above-described fort, if it merited that name, was, when the siege commenced, in the condition for defense in which it had been left by the Mexican general; Cos, when he capitulated in the fall of 1835. The chapel, except the west end and north projection, had been unroofed, the east end being occupied by the platform of earth...twelve feet high, with a slope for ascension to the west. On its level were mounted three pieces of cannon. One (1), a twelve-pounder, pointed east through an embrasure roughly notched in the wall; another (2) was aimed north through a similar notch; and another (3) fired over the wall to the south. High scaffolds of wood enabled marksmen to use the top of the roofless wall as a parapet. The entrenchment...consisted of a ditch and breastwork, the latter of earth packed between two rows of palisades, the outer row being higher than the earthwork. Behind it and near the gate was a battery of four guns...,all four-pounders, pointing south. The *porte-cochere* through the low barrack was covered on the outside by a lunette of stockades and earth, mounted with two guns....In the southwest angle of the large area was an eighteen-pounder...,and east of this, within the north wall, two more guns of the same caliber....All the guns of this area were mounted on high platforms of stockades and earth, and fired over the walls. The several barriers were covered on the outside with a ditch, except where such guard was afforded by the irrigating canal, which flowed on the east and west sides of the fort....

The besieging force [was] now around the Alamo....[S]ix battalions of foot were to form the storming forces....The infantry were directed at a certain hour between midnight and dawn to form at convenient distances from the fort in four columns of attack.... A certain number of scaling ladders, axes, and fascines were to be borne by particular columns. A commanding officer, with a second to replace him in case of accident, was named, and a point of attack designated for each column. The cavalry were to be stationed at suitable points around the fort to cut off fugitives....Santa Ana [Potter's spelling] took his station, with a part of his staff and all the bands of music at a battery about five hundred yards south of the Alamo and near the old bridge, from which post a signal was to be given by a bugle-note for the columns to move simultaneously at double-quick time against the fort. One,...commanded by Castrillon, was to rush through the breach on the north; another, commanded by General Cos, was to storm the chapel; and a third...was to scale the west barrier. Cos, who had evacuated San Antonio the year before under capitulation, was assigned to the most difficult point of attack, probably to give him an opportunity to retrieve his standing. By the timing of the signal it was calculated that the columns would reach the foot of the wall just as it should become sufficiently light for good operation.

When the hour came, the south guns of the Alamo were answering the batteries which fronted them; but the music was silent till the blast of a bugle was followed by the rushing tramp of soldiers. The guns of the fort opened upon the moving masses, and Santa Ana's bands struck up the assassin note of *deguello*, or no quarter.

But a few and not very effective discharges of cannon from the works could be made before the enemy were under them, and it was probably not till then that the worn and wearied garrison was fully mustered. Castrillon's column arrived first at the foot of the wall, but was not the first to enter. The guns of the north, where Travis commanded in person, probably raked the breach, and this or the fire of the riflemen brought the column to a disordered halt, and Colonel Duque, who commanded the battalion of Toluca, fell dangerously wounded; but while this was occurring the column from the west crossed the barrier on that side by escalade at a point north of the center. As this checked resistance at the north, Castrillon shortly afterward passed the breach. It was probably while the enemy was thus pouring into the large area that Travis fell at his post, for his body, with a single shot in the forehead, was found beside the gun at the northwest angle. The outer walls and batteries, all except one gun,...were now abandoned by the defenders. In the meantime Cos had again proved unlucky. His column was repulsed from the chapel, and his troops fell back in disorder behind the old stone stable and huts that stood south of the southwest angle. There they were soon rallied and led into the large area by General Amador....

This all passed within a few minutes after the bugle sounded. The garrison, when driven from the thinly manned outer defences, whose early loss was inevitable, took refuge in the buildings before described, but mainly in the long barrack; and it was not until then, when they became more concentrated and covered within, that the main struggle began....[T]here was no communicating between buildings, nor, in all cases, between rooms. There was little need of command, however....There was now no retreating from point to point, and each group of defenders had to fight and die in the den where it was brought to bay. From the doors, windows, and loopholes of the several rooms around the area the crack of the rifle and the hiss of the bullet came thick and fast....The gun beside which Travis fell was now turned against the buildings, as were also some others, and shot after shot was sent crashing through the doors and barricades of the several rooms. Each ball was followed by a storm of musketry and a charge; and thus room after room was carried at the point of the bayonet, when all within them died fighting to the last....

The chapel, which was the last point taken, was carried by a *coup de main* after the fire of the other buildings was silenced. Once the enemy was in possession of the large area, the guns of the south could be turned to fire into the door of the church, only from fifty to a hundred yards off, and that was probably the route of attack. The inmates of this last stronghold, like the rest, fought to the last, and continued to fire down from the upper works after the enemy occupied the floor....Towards the close of the struggle Lieutenant Dickinson, with his child in his arms, or as some accounts say, tied to his back, leaped from the east embrasure of the chapel, and both were shot in the act. Of those he left behind him, the bayonet soon gleaned what the bullet had left....

The action, according to Santa Ana's report, lasted thirty minutes. It was certainly short, and possibly no longer time passed between the moment the enemy entered the breach and that when resistance died out. The assault was a task which had to be carried out quickly or fail. Some of the incidents which have to be related separately occurred simultaneously, and all occupied very little

Susanna Dickinson
(Library of Congress)

time....About the time the area was entered, a few men, cut off from inward retreat, leaped from the barriers, and attempted flight, but were all sabered or speared by the cavalry except one who succeeded in hiding himself under a small bridge of the irrigating ditch. There he was discovered and reported a few hours after by some laundresses engaged in washing near the spot. He was executed. Half an hour or more after the action was over a few men were found concealed in one of the rooms under some mattresses....The officer to whom the discovery was first reported entreated Santa Ana to spare their lives; but he was sternly rebuked, and the men ordered to be shot, which was done....

The negro belonging to Travis, the wife of Lieutenant Dickinson,...and a few Mexican women with their children were the only inmates of the fort whose lives were spared. The massacre involved no women and but one child. Lieutenant Dickinson commanded the gun at the east embrasure of the chapel. His family was probably in one of the small vaulted rooms of the north projection, which will account for his being able to take his child to the rear of the building when it was being stormed. An irrigating canal ran below the embrasure, and his aim may have been to break the shock of his leap by landing in the mud of that waterless ditch, and then try to escape; or he may have thought that so striking an act would plead for his life; but the shower of bullets which greeted him told how vain was the hope. The authenticity of this highly dramatic incident has been questioned, but it was asserted from the first, and was related to me by an eyewitness engaged in the assault.

Eyewitnesses

De la Peña, born in 1807 and educated as a mining engineer, held the rank of lieutenant colonel in Mexico's Sapper Battalion. His handwritten diary, covering October 8, 1835, through June 11, 1836, was published originally in 1837. It has been called a fake because his military record is blank for that period, perhaps removed because of his criticism of Santa Anna for poor provisions and inept military actions. Very observant of the countryside, he lamented the loss of a territory with so much potential. De la Peña died penniless in 1842 after backing General Urrea's bid to reestablish a constitutional government.

Source: José Enrique de la Peña, *With Santa Anna in Texas: A Personal Narrative of the Revolution*, translated and edited by Carmen Perry with an introduction by Llerena Friend (College Station: Texas A & M University Press, 1975), pp. 6-57. Reprinted by permission of Texas A&M University Press.

War was the thing that could least frighten Mexicans, who seemed to have sworn not to live without it, but the distance of the country in which it would be waged, its climate, and the local conditions …were factors of considerable weight in the eyes of the thinking person.…

In an immense, open, and uninhabited country, it was necessary to take everything along and to proceed in a manner heretofore unknown.…[T]his particular phase of it was done in a fashion so offensive to humanity as to appear incredible.…General Cos had been hemmed in at Béjar, 480 leagues from the capital.…[H]e was compelled to capitulate on the 10th of December 1835.…

General Ramírez y Sesma received order to come to the aid of General Cos.…

On the 26th of December Ramírez y Sesma's division joined with that of General Cos, who had already arrived at Laredo following the capitulation at Béjar.…

The enemy did not expect our forces until the middle of March. ...He expected us to march on Goliad, the key position that would have opened the door to the principal theater of war. In fact, we should have attacked the enemy at the heart instead of weakening ourselves by going to Béjar....[T]he commander in chief heard it from all those of any significance in the army; but...he disdained their approval....General Santa Anna becomes irritable with discussions....

With the intention of joining the Sapper Battalion,...I left Monclova....We had set out with a fierce norther and had suffered all day long, facing its cutting winds and rain, and by seven that night the rain had turned to snow....Our soldiers, especially the cavalrymen, suffered cruelly from the intense cold, so foreign to them and for which their clothing was not suitable....

On the 27th [of February]...a message arrived from the commander in chief. He communicated that on the 23rd he had entered Béjar and that the enemy had retreated and had barricaded themselves in the fortress of the Alamo. He ordered the sapper battalions from Aldama and Toluca to start forced marches....

On the 3rd of March between eight and nine in the morning, after the troops had put on their dress uniforms, we marched toward Béjar, entering between four and five in the afternoon within sight of the enemy, who observed us from inside their fortifications....

[O]n the 5th the order was given for the assault....

Beginning at one o'clock in the morning of the 6th, the columns were set in motion, and at three they silently advanced toward the river, which they crossed marching two abreast over some narrow wooden bridges....Silence was again ordered and smoking was prohibited. The moon was up, but the density of the clouds that covered it allowed only an opaque light in our direction....Light began to appear on the horizon;...a bugle call to attention was the agreed signal and we soon heard that terrible bugle call of death....

Alerted to our attack by the given signal, which all columns answered, the enemy vigorously returned our fire, which had not

even touched him but had retarded our advance. Travis, to compensate for the reduced number of the defenders, had placed three or four rifles by the side of each man, so that the initial fire was very rapid and deadly. Our columns left along their path a wide trail of blood, of wounded, and of dead....

The columns, bravely storming the fort in the midst of a terrible shower of bullets and cannon-fire, had reached the base of the walls....The few poor ladders that we were bringing had not arrived, because their bearers had either perished on the way or had escaped....A lively rifle fire coming from the roof of the barracks and other points caused painful havoc, increasing the confusion of our disorderly mass....The sharp reports of the rifles, the whistling of bullets, the groans of the wounded, the cursing of the men, the sighs and anguished cries of the dying, the arrogant harangues of the officers, the noise of the instrument of war, and the inordinate shouts of the attackers, who climbed vigorously, bewildered all and made of this moment a tremendous and critical one. The shouting of those being attacked was no less loud and from the beginning had pierced our ears with desperate, terrible cries of alarm in a language we did not understand....

A quarter of an hour had elapsed, during which our soldiers remained in a terrible situation, wearing themselves out as they climbed in quest of a less obscure death than that visited on them; ...later and after much effort, they were able in sufficient numbers to reach the parapet....The terrified defenders withdrew at once into quarters....Not all of them took refuge, for some remained in the open, looking at us before firing. Travis was seen to hesitate, but not about the death that he would choose. He would take a few steps and stop, turning his proud face toward us to discharge his shots; he fought like a true soldier. Finally he died, but he died after having traded his life very dearly....

Our soldiers...burst into the quarters where the enemy had entrenched themselves, from which issued an infernal fire. Behind these came others, who nearing the doors and blind with fury and smoke, fired their shots against friends and enemies alike....

Among the defenders there were thirty or more colonists; the rest were pirates....The order had been given to spare no one but the women and this was carried out, but such carnage was useless; and had we prevented it, we would have saved much blood on our part. Those of the enemy who tried to escape fell victims to the sabers of the cavalry, which had been drawn up for this purpose, but even as they fled they defended themselves. An unfortunate father with a young son in his arms was seen to hurl himself from a considerable height, both perishing at the same blow.

This scene of extermination went on for an hour before the curtain of death covered and ended it: shortly after six in the morning it was all finished....The bodies, with their blackened and bloody faces disfigured by a desperate death, their hair and uniform burning at once, presented a dreadful and truly hellish sight. What trophies — those of the battlefield!...The enemy could be identified by their whiteness, by their robust and bulky shapes....

The general then addressed his crippled battalions, lauding their courage and thanking them in the name of their country....

Shortly before Santa Anna's speech, an unpleasant episode had taken place, which, since it occurred after the end of the skirmish, was looked upon as base murder....Some seven men had survived the general carnage and, under the protection of General Castrillón, they were brought before Santa Anna. Among them was one of great stature, well proportioned, with regular features, in whose face there was the imprint of adversity, but in whom one also noticed a degree of resignation and nobility that did him honor. He was the naturalist David Crockett, well known in North America for his unusual adventures, who had undertaken to explore the country and who, finding himself in Béjar at the very moment of surprise, had taken refuge in the Alamo, fearing that his status as a foreigner might not be respected. Santa Anna answered Castrillón's intervention in Crockett's behalf with a gesture of indignation and, addressing himself to the sappers, the troops closest to them, ordered his execution. The commanders and officers were outraged at this action and did not support the order, hoping that once the fury of the moment had blown over these men would be spared, but several officers were around the president and who, perhaps, had not been present during the moment of danger, became noteworthy by an infamous deed....They thrust themselves forward, in order to flatter their commander, and with swords in hand, fell upon these unfortunate, defenseless men....Though tortured before they were killed, these unfortunates died without complaining and without humiliation themselves....I turned away horrified in order not to witness such a barbarous scene....

Death united in one place both friends and enemies; within a few hours a funeral pyre rendered into ashes those men who moments before had been so brave that in a blind fury they had unselfishly offered their lives and had met their ends in combat. The greater part of our dead were buried by their comrades, but the enemy, who seems to have some respect for the dead, attributed the great pyre of their dead to our hatred....

The responsibility for the victims sacrificed at the Alamo must rest on General Ramírez y Sesma rather than on the commander in chief. He knew that the enemy was at Béjar in small numbers. ...When General Ramírez y Sesma sighted the town, the enemy was still engaged in the pleasures of a dance given the night before. ...Had he just placed himself at the bridge over the San Antonio that connects the fort to the city, as he was advised, he would have prevented the enemy from taking refuge there, thus avoiding the painful catastrophe that we witnessed.

Juana Navarro Pérez Alsbury was in the Alamo during the battle. A niece of José Antonio Navarro, she had been adopted by Governor Juan Martín Veramendi, James Bowie's father-in-law. As the Mexican force approached, her husband, Dr. Horatio Alexander Alsbury, was away, and it was probably because of Bowie that she entered the Alamo with her sister, Gertrudis. After the battle, she talked with a brother-in-law who was in the Mexican army, but she does not mention meeting Santa Anna, although he reportedly interviewed all the women before they were released.

Death of Bowie. Painting by Louis Eyth. (The Daughters of the Republic of Texas Library. CN95.229)

44

This account, recorded some fifty years after the battle, is among the thirteen hundred handwritten pages of "Rip" Ford's memoirs. Ford arrived at the beginning of the Republic, chronicled major events in which he participated, and interviewed participants about those he had not witnessed.

Source: John S[almon] Ford, "Mrs. Alsbury's Recollections of the Alamo," pp. 102-4 in *Memoirs of John S. Ford and Reminiscences of Texas History from 1836 to 1888*, ca. 1885-97, unpublished manuscript, The Center for American History, The University of Texas at Austin. Courtesy of The Center for American History, The University of Texas at Austin.

...On leaving he [Bowie] said: "Sister, do not be afraid. I leave you with Colonel Travis, Colonel Crockett, and other friends. They are gentlemen and will treat you kindly." He had himself brought back two or three times to see and talk with her. Their last interview took place three or four days before the fall of the Alamo. She never saw him again, either alive or dead.

She says she does not know who nursed him after he left the quarters she occupied and expresses no disbelief in the statement of Madam Candelaria [Andrea Castañón Villanueva]. "There were people in the Alamo I did not see." [*Editor's note. Madam Candelaria, whose presence at the Alamo has been contested, claimed that Bowie died in her arms only a few minutes before soldiers burst into the room to which he had gone, ill and weakened.*]

Mrs. Alsbury and her sister...saw very little of the fighting. While the final struggle was progressing she peeped out and saw the surging columns of Santa Anna assaulting the Alamo on every side, as she believed. She could hear the noise of the conflict — the roar of the artillery, the rattle of the small arms, the shouts of the combatants, the groans of the dying, and the moans of the wounded....[S]he realized the fact that the brave Texians had been overwhelmed by numbers. She asked her sister to go to the door and request the Mexican soldiers not to fire into the room, as it contained women only. Señorita Gertrudis opened the door, she was greeted in offensive language by the soldiers. Her shawl was torn from her shoulders and she rushed back into the room. During this period Mrs. Alsbury was standing with her one-year-old son strained to her bosom, supposing he would be motherless soon. The soldiers then demanded of Señorita Gertrudis: "Your money and your husband." She replied: "I have neither money nor husband." About this time a sick man ran up to Mrs. Alsbury and attempted to protect her. The soldiers bayoneted him at her side. She thinks his name was Mitchell....

The soldiers broke open her trunk and took her money and clothes, also the watch of Colonel Travis and other officers.

A Mexican officer appeared on the scene. He excitedly inquired, "How did you come here? What are you doing here any how? Where is the entrance to the fort?" He made her pass out of the room over a cannon standing nearby the door. He told her to remain there and he would have her sent to President Santa Anna. Another officer came up and asked: "What are you doing here?" She replied: "An officer ordered us to remain here and he would have us sent to the President." "President the devil. Don't you see they are about to fire that cannon? Leave." They were moving when they heard a voice calling "Sister." "To my great relief Don Manuel Pérez came to us. He said: 'Don't you know your own brother-in-law?' I answered: 'I am so excited and distressed that I scarcely know anything.'" Don Manuel placed them in charge of a colored woman belonging to Colonel Bowie and the party reached the house of Don Angel Navarro in safety....

She describes Colonel Bowie as a tall, well made gentleman, of a very serious countenance, of few words, always to the point, and a warm friend. In his family he was affectionate, kind, and so acted as to secure the love and confidence of all.

Enrique Esparza, a young San Antonio native went into the Alamo with his family as Mexican troops approached. He was probably eight but maybe twelve. The events he describes were recorded seventy years later.

Source: Enrique Esparza, "Alamo's Only Survivor," interview by Charles Merritt Barnes, *San Antonio Express*, May 12 and May 19, 1907, quoted in Timothy M. Matovina, *The Alamo Remembered: Tejano Accounts and Perspectives* (Austin: University of Texas Press, 1995), pp. 77-89.

...I am the son of Gregorio Esparza.

You will see my father's name on the list of those who died in the Alamo....

My mother was also in the Alamo when it fell, as were some of my brothers and a sister....

Santa Anna and his army arrived at about sundown and almost immediately after we sought refuge in the Alamo....

It was twilight when we got into the Alamo and it grew pitch dark soon afterward. All of the doors were closed and barred....

I distinctly remember that I climbed through the window and over a cannon that was placed inside of the church immediately behind the window. There were several other cannon there....

We had not been in there long when a messenger came from Santa Anna calling on us to surrender. I remember the reply to this summons was a shot from one of the cannon on the roof of the Alamo. Soon after it was fired I heard Santa Anna's cannon reply....

The end came [nearly two weeks later] suddenly and almost unexpectedly and with a rush....

After all had been dark and quiet for many hours and I had fallen into a profound slumber suddenly there was a terrible din. Cannon boomed. Their shot crashed through the doors and windows and the breeches in the wall. Then men rushed in on us. They swarmed among us and over us. After the soldiers of Santa Anna had got in a corner all of the women and children who had not been killed in the onslaught, they kept firing on the men who had defended the Alamo....

The last I saw of my father's corpse was when one of them held his lantern above it and over the dead who lay about the cannon he had tended....

After all of the men had been slain, the women and children were kept huddled up in the church's southwest corner in the small room to the right of the large double door of the church as one enters it. A guard was put over them. They were held there until after daylight when orders were given to remove them. We were all marched off to the house of Señor Músquiz [chief official of San Antonio]. Here all of the women were again placed under guard....My mother and father were well acquainted with the Músquiz family. At about eight o'clock we became very hungry, up to then not having been given any food. My mother, being familiar with the premises, began to look about for food for herself and children as well as her other comrades. While she was doing so Músquiz told her that it was dangerous for her to be moving about and leaving the place and room in which she was under guard. She told him she did not care whether she was under guard or not, she was going to have something to eat for herself, her children and her companions whom she intended to feed if Santa Anna did not feed his prisoners. Músquiz admonished her to silence and told her to be patient and he would get them some food from his own store....

[H]e got quite a quantity of provisions and brought them to the room in which the prisoners, some ten or a dozen in number, were and distributed the food among them. There was some coffee as well as bread and meat. I recollect that I ate heartily, but my mother very sparingly.

We were kept at Músquiz's house until three o'clock in the afternoon when the prisoners were taken to Military Plaza....

Mrs. Alsbury and her sister, Mrs. Gertrude Cantú, were the first ones to be taken before Santa Anna. He questioned them and, after talking with them for a few minutes, discharged them from custody and they left....

Mrs. Dickinson, the wife of Lieutenant Dickinson, the woman

whom I told you, like my mother, had a babe at her breast, was the next to be summoned before Santa Anna. He spent some time in questioning her after which he dismissed her.

My mother was next called before the dictator. When she appeared before him my baby sister pressed closely to her bosom. I with my brother followed her into his presence. My brother was clinging to her skirt, but I stood to one side and behind her. I watched every move and listened to every word spoken. Santa Anna asked her name. She gave it. He then asked, "Where is your husband?"

She answered, sobbing: "He's dead at the Alamo."

Santa Anna next asked where the other members of the family were. She replied a brother of my father's, she was informed, was in his [Santa Anna's] army. This was true. My father had a brother whose name was Francisco Esparza, who joined the forces of Santa Anna. It was this brother who appeared before Santa Anna later and asked permission to search among the slain for my father's corpse. The permission was given. My uncle found my father's body and had it buried in the *campo santo* [cemetery] where Milam Square is now. I did not get a chance to see it before it was buried there as the burial, as all others incident to that battle, was a very hurried one. It is probable that my father was the only one who fought on the side of the Constitutionalists and against the forces of the dictator whose body was buried without having first been burned.

Santa Anna released my mother. He gave her a blanket and two silver dollars as he dismissed her. I was informed that he gave a blanket and the same sum of money to each of the other women who were brought from the Alamo before him....

After our release we went back to our home and my mother wept for many days and nights. I frequently went to the Main Plaza and watched the soldiers of Santa Anna and saw him quite a number of times before they marched away toward Houston where he was defeated.

Yorba was in her nineties when she gave this interview relating her memories of attending wounded Mexican soldiers after the Alamo was taken. Her claim that everyone knew when the assault would take place is not accurate, but her physical description of Crockett is.

Source: Eulalia Yorba, "Another Story of the Alamo," interview, *San Antonio Express*, April 12, 1896, quoted in Timothy M. Matovina *The Alamo Remembered: Tejano Accounts and Perspectives* (Austin: University of Texas Press, 1995), pp. 53-7.

I well remember when Santa Anna and his two thousand soldiers on horses and with shining muskets and bayonets marched into the little pueblo of San Antonio. The news ran from mouth to mouth that Colonel Travis, Davy Crockett and Colonel Bowie and the 160 or so other Texans who had held that locality against the Mexicans for several weeks had taken refuge in and had barricaded themselves in that old stone mission, which had been used as a crude fort or garrison long before I came to the country. It belonged to Mexico and a few stands of muskets and three or four cannons were kept there. When Santa Anna's army came they camped on the plains about the pueblo and a guard was put about the Alamo fort. That was from the last day of February to March 4. Of course, I kept at home with my little boys and never stirred out once, for we women were all terribly frightened. Every eatable in the house, all the cows, lumber and hay about the place were taken by the troops, but we were assured that if we remained in the house no personal harm would come to us.

Of course, we were hourly informed of the news. We knew that the Texans in the Alamo were surrounded by over five hundred soldiers constantly, while fifteen hundred more soldiers were in camp out on the plains. We learned that four days had been given the Texans to surrender. We heard from the soldiers that not one of the imprisoned men had so much as returned a reply to the demand for surrender and that on the morning of the 6th of March 1836, Santa Anna was going to bring matters to a crisis with the beleaguered rebels. I never can tell the anxiety that we people on the outside felt for that mere handful of men in the old fort, when we saw around hostile troops as far as we could see and not a particle of help for the Texans, for whom we few residents of the town had previously formed a liking.

The morning of Sunday — the 6th of March — ah! indeed, I could never forget that, even if I lived many years more—was clear and balmy and every scrap of food was gone from my house and the children and I ran to the home of a good old Spanish priest so that we could have food and comfort there. There was nothing to impede the view of the Alamo from the priest's home, although I wished there was. The shooting began at six in the morning. It seemed as if there were myriads of soldiers and guns about the stone building. There was volley after volley fired into the barred and bolted windows. Then the volleys came in quick succession. Occasionally we heard muffled volleys and saw puffs of smoke from within the Alamo, and when we saw, too, Mexican soldiers fall in the roadway or stagger back we knew the Texans were fighting as best they could for their lives.

It seemed as if ten thousand guns were shot off indiscriminately as firecrackers snap when whole bundles of them are set off at one time. The smoke grew thick and heavy and we could not see clearly down at the Alamo, while the din of musketry, screams of crazy, exultant Mexicans increased every moment. I have never heard human beings scream so fiercely and powerfully as the Mexican soldiers that day. I can compare such screams only to the yell of a mountain panther or lynx in desperate straits.

Next several companies of soldiers came running down the street with great heavy bridge timbers. These were quickly brought to bear as battering rams on the mission doors, but several volleys from within the Alamo, as nearly as we could see, laid low the men at the timbers and stopped the battering for a short time. Three or four brass cannons were loaded with what seemed to us very long delay and were placed directly in front of the main doors of the mission. They did serious work. Meanwhile, bullets from several thousand muskets incessantly rained like hail upon the building and went through the apertures that had been made in the wood barricades at the windows and doors. The din was indescribable. It did not seem as if a mouse could live in a building so shot at and riddled as the Alamo was that morning.

Next we saw ladders brought and in a trice the low roof of the church was crowded with a screaming, maddened throng of men armed with guns and sabers. Of course we knew then that it was all up with the little band of men in the Alamo. I remember that the priest drew us away from the window and refused to let us look longer, notwithstanding the fascination of the scene. We could still hear the shouts and yells and the booming of the brass cannon shook the priest's house and rattled the window panes.

Along about nine o'clock, I should judge, the shooting and swearing and yelling had ceased, but the air was thick and heavy with blue powder smoke. A Mexican colonel came running to the priest's residence and asked that we go down to the Alamo to do what we could for the dying men.

Such a dreadful sight. The roadway was thronged with Mexican soldiers with smoke and dirt begrimed faces, haggard eyes and wild, insane expression. There were twelve or fifteen bodies of Mexicans lying dead and bleeding here and there and others were being carried to an adobe house across the way. The stones in the church wall were spotted with blood, the doors were splintered and battered in. Pools of thick blood were so frequent on the sun-baked earth about the stone building that we had to be careful to avoid stepping in them. There was a din of excited voices along the street and the officers were marshaling their men for moving to camp.

But no one could even tell you the horror of the scene that met our gaze when we were led by the sympathetic little colonel into the old Alamo to bandage up the wounds of several young men there. I used to try when I was younger to describe that awful sight, but I never could find sufficient language. There were only a few Mexicans in there when we came and they were all officers who had ordered the common soldiers away from the scene of death and — yes — slaughter, for that was what it was. The floor was literally crimson with blood. The woodwork all about us was riddled and splintered by lead balls and what was left of the old altar at the rear of the church was cut and slashed by cannon ball and bullets. The air was dark with powder smoke and was hot and heavy. The odor was oppressive and sickening and the simply horrible scene nerved us as nothing else could.

The dead Texans lay singly and in heaps of three or four, or in irregular rows here and there all about the floor of the Alamo, just as they had fallen when a ball reached a vital part or they had dropped to their death from loss of blood. Of course we went to work as soon as we got to the mission at helping the bleeding and moaning men, who had only a few hours at most more of life; but the few minutes that we looked upon the corpses all about us gave a picture that has always been as distinct as one before my very eyes.

So thick were the bodies of the dead that we had to step over them to get [near] a man in whom there was still life. Close to my feet was a young man who had been shot through the forehead. He had dropped dead with his eyes staring wildly open and, as he lay there, seemingly gazed up into my face.

I remember seeing poor old Colonel Davy Crockett as he lay dead by the side of a dying man, whose bloody and powder-stained face I was washing. Colonel Crockett was about fifty years old at that time. His coat and rough woolen shirt were soaked with blood so that the original color was hidden, for the eccentric hero must have died of some ball in the chest or a bayonet thrust.

David Crockett. He is often called Davy Crockett.
(Photograph of painting by William H. Huddle)

Villanueva, part of Seguin's company, was in San Antonio during the fight at the Alamo. In a deposition to support the petition of Gregorio Esparza's heirs to receive veterans' benefits, he identifies at least four Tejanos who fought on the side of the Texans.

Source: Candelario Villanueva, deposition, August 26, 1859, quoted in Timothy M. Matovina *The Alamo Remembered: Tejano Accounts and Perspectives*, (Austin: University of Texas Press, 1995), pp. 35-6.

The State of Texas, County of Béxar

Before me, Samuel S. Smith, Clerk of the County Court of said county, personally appeared Candelario Villanueva, a citizen of Béxar to me personally known, who being by me first duly sworn upon his oath saith that he was a member of Captain Juan N. Seguín's Company in 1835 and 1836. That he entered Béxar between the mornings of the 5th and 10th of December 1835 with the American forces; that the late Gregorio Esparza was also a soldier of Captain Juan N. Seguín's Company and he did enter Béxar with the American forces and actually assisted in the reduction of Béxar and that he remained therein till after the capitulation of General Cos. Subsequently after the storming of Béxar the said Gregorio Esparza remained at Béxar until the approach of Santa Anna's army when he went into the Alamo with the Americans.

I [Villanueva] remained at Béxar and when Santa Anna's troops were entering the town I started with Colonel Seguín for the Alamo, when we were on the way Colonel Seguín sent me back to lock his house up; whilst performing that duty Santa Anna's soldiers got between me and the Alamo and I had to remain in the town during the siege and assault of the Alamo. After the fall of the Alamo I went there and among the dead bodies of those lying inside of the rooms I recognized the body of Gregorio Esparza; I also saw the dead bodies of Antonio Fuentes, Toribio Losoya, Guadalupe Rodríguez and other Mexicans who had fallen in the defense of the Alamo, as also the bodies of Colonel Travis, Bowie, Crockett and other Americans that I had previously known. I saw Francisco Esparza and his brothers take the body of Gregorio Esparza and carry it off towards the *campo santo* [cemetery] for interment; the bodies of the Americans were laid in a pile and burnt. I remained in Béxar until the return of Captain Seguín and his companions after the battle of San Jacinto when I rejoined his company.

Aftermath

Ruiz, mayor of San Antonio during Santa Anna's occupation, was the son of a signer of the Texas Declaration of Independence. Immediately after the Alamo was overrun, Santa Anna ordered him to bury the Mexicans who had been killed and to burn the bodies of the Texans.

Source: Francis [Francisco] Antonio Ruiz, "Fall of the Alamo, and Massacre of Travis and his Brave Associates," translated by J. A. Quintero, *The Texas Almanac for 1860*, pp. 80-81, quoted in Amelia Williams, "A Critical Study of the Siege of the Alamo and of the Personnel of Its Defenders," *Southwestern Historical Quarterly*, 37, no. 1 (July 1933), pp. 39-40.

On the 6th of March, at 3 a.m., General Santa Anna at the head of 4,000 men advanced against the Alamo. The infantry, artillery, and cavalry had formed about 1000 varas from the walls of the same fortress. The Mexican army charged and were twice repulsed by the deadly fire of Travis's artillery, which resembled a constant thunder. At the third charge the Toluca battalion commenced to scale the walls and suffered severely. Out of 830 men, only 130 of the battalion were [left] alive.

When the Mexican army entered the walls, I with the Political Chief, Don Ramon Musquiz and other members of the corporation, accompanied the curate, Don Refugio de la Garza, who by Santa Anna's orders had assembled during the night at a temporary fortification on Potrero Street, with the object of attending the wounded, etc. As soon as the storming commenced we crossed the bridge on Commerce Street with this object in view and about 100 yards from the same a party of Mexican dragoons fired upon us and compelled us to fall back on the river to the place that we had occupied before. Half an hour had elapsed when Santa Anna sent one of his aides-de-camp with an order for us to come before him. He directed me to call on some of the neighbors to come with carts to carry the (Mexican) dead to the [cemetery], and to accompany him, as he desired to have Colonels Travis, Bowie, and Crockett shown to him.

On the north battery of the fortress convent, lay the lifeless body of Col. Travis on the gun carriage, shot only through the forehead. Toward the west and in the small fort opposite the city, we found the body of Colonel Crockett. Col. Bowie was found dead in his bed in one of the rooms on the south side.

Santa Anna, after all the Mexican bodies were taken out, ordered wood to be brought to burn the bodies of the Texans. He sent a company of dragoons with me to bring wood and dry branches from the neighboring forests. About three o'clock in the afternoon on March 6, we laid the wood and dry branches upon which a file of dead bodies was placed, more wood was piled on them, them another pile of bodies was brought, and in this manner they were all arranged in layers. Kindling wood was distributed through the pile and about 5 o'clock in the evening it was lighted.

The dead Mexicans of Santa Anna were taken to the grave-yard, but not having sufficient room for them, I ordered some of them to be thrown in the river, which was done on the same day.

The gallantry of the few Texans who defended the Alamo was really wondered at by the Mexican army. Even the generals were astonished at their vigorous resistance, and how dearly victory was bought.

The generals under Santa Anna who participated in the storming of the Alamo, were Juan Amador, Castrillon, Ramirez y Sesma, and Andrade.

The men (Texans) burnt numbered one hundred eighty-two. I was an eyewitness, for as alcalde of San Antonio I was with some of the neighbors, collecting the dead bodies and placing them on the funeral pyre.

Francis Antonio Ruiz

Sequín, as military commander in San Antonio, was given responsibility of burying the ashes of the Texans killed at the Alamo. At the ceremony that took place almost exactly a year after the siege began, Sequín delivered a patriotic speech in Spanish. Two weeks later, he wrote General Albert Sidney Johnston of his actions.

Sources: Juan N. Sequín to General Albert Sidney Johnston, March 13, 1837 and "Juan Sequín's Address at the Burial of the Alamo Defenders, Béxar, February 25, 1837," quoted in Jesús de la Teja, editor, *A Revolution Remembered: The Memoirs and Selected Correspondence of Juan N. Sequín* (Austin: State House Press, 1991), pp. 162, 156.

From Sequín's Letter to General Johnston

... In conformity with the orders from Genl. Felix Huston dated some time back, I caused the honors of war to be paid to the remains of the Heroes of Alamo on the 25th of Feby last. The ashes were found in three heaps. I caused a coffin to be prepared neatly covered with black, the ashes from the two smallest heaps were placed therein and with a view to attach additional solemnity to the occasion were carried to the Parish Church in Béxar whence it moved with the procession at 4 O'Clock on the afternoon of the day above mentioned. The Procession passed through the principal street of the city, crossed the River and passing through the principal avenue arrived at the spot whence part of the ashes had been collected, the procession halted, the coffin was placed upon the spot, and three volleys of musquetry wer [sic] discharged over it by one of the companies, proceeding onwards to the second spot from whence the ashes were taken where the same honors were done and thence to the principal spot and place of interment [sic], the coffin was then placed upon the large heap of ashes when I addressed a few words to the Battallion [sic] and assemblage present in honor of the occasion in the Castillian language as I do not possess the English. Major Western then addressed the concourse in the latter tongue, the coffin and all the ashes were then interred and three volleys of musquetry were fired over the grave by the whole Battallion [sic] with an accuracy that would do honor to the best disciplined troops. We then marched back to quarter in the city with music and colors flying. Half hour guns were not fired because I had no powder for the purpose, but every honor was done within the reach of my scanty means. I hope as a whole my efforts may meet your approbation....

> I have the honor to be
> Very Respecty. yr. obt. Sert.
> John N. Seguin
> Lieut. Col. Commg.

Sequín's speech at the ceremony

Companions in Arms!! These remains which we have the honor of carrying on our shoulders are those of the valiant heroes who died in the Alamo. Yes, my friends, they preferred to die a thousand times rather than submit themselves to the tyrant's yoke. What a brilliant example! Deserving of being noted in the pages of history. The spirit of liberty appears to be looking out from its elevated throne with its pleasing mien and pointing to us, saying: "there are your brothers, Travis, Bowie, Crockett, and others whose valor places them in the rank of my heroes." Yes soldiers and fellow citizens, these are the worthy beings who, by the twists of fate, during the present campaign delivered their bodies to the ferocity of their enemies; who, barbarously treated as beasts, were bound by their feet and dragged to this spot, where they were reduced to ashes. The venerable remains of our worthy companions as witnesses, I invite you to declare to the entire world, "Texas shall be free and independent, or we shall perish in glorious combat."

Defenders of the Alamo

This roster of 189 who died defending the Alamo has evolved over the years.

Source: The Daughters of the Republic of Texas, "The Story of the Alamo: Thirteen Fateful Days," undated pamphlet, [San Antonio].

Juan Abamillo, San Antonio
R. Allen
Mills DeForrest Andross, Vermont
Micajah Autry, N.C.
Juan A. Badillo, San Antonio
Peter James Bailey, Ky.
Isaac G. Baker, Ark.
William Charles M. Baker, Mo.
John J. Ballentine
Richard W. Ballantine, Scotland
John J. Baugh, Va.
Joseph Bayliss, Tenn.
John Blair, Tenn.
Samuel C. Blair, Tenn.
William Blazeby, England
James Butler Bonham, S.C.
Daniel Bourne, England
James Bowie, Tenn.
Jesse B. Bowman
George Brown, England
James Brown, Pa.
Robert Brown
James Buchanan, Ala.
Samuel E. Burns, Ireland
George D. Butler, Mo.
Robert Campbell, Tenn.
John Cane, Pa.
William R. Carey, Va.
Charles Henry Clark, Mo.
M.B. Clark
Daniel William Cloud, Ky.
Robert E. Cochran, N.J.
George Washington Cottle, Tenn.
Henry Courtman, Germany
Lemuel Crawford, S.C.
David Crockett, Tenn.
Robert Crossman, Mass.
David P. Cummings, Pa.
Robert Cunningham, N.Y.
Jacob C. Darst, Ky.

John Davis, Ky.
Freeman H. K. Day
Jerry C. Day, Mo.
Squire Daymon, Tenn.
William Dearduff, Tenn.
Stephen Dennison, England
Charles Despallier, La.
Almeron Dickinson, Tenn.
John H. Dillard, Tenn.
James R. Dimpkins, England
Lewis Duel, N.Y.
Andrew Duvalt, Ireland
Carlos Espalier, San Antonio
Gregorio Esparza, San Antonio
Robert Evans, Ireland
Samuel B. Evans, N.Y.
James L. Ewing, Tenn.
William Fishbaugh, Ala.
John Flanders, Mass.
Dolphin Ward Floyd, N.C.
John Hubbard Forsyth, N.Y.
Antonio Fuentes, San Antonio
Galba Fuqua, Ala.
William H. Furtleroy, Ky.
William Garnett, Tenn.
James W. Garrand, La.
James Girard Garrett, Tenn.
John E. Garvin
John E. Gaston, Ky.
James George
John Camp Goodrich, Tenn.
Albert Calvin Grimes, Ga.
Jose Maria Guerrero, Laredo, Tex.
James C. Gwynne, England
James Hannum
John Harris, Ky.
Andrew Jackson Harrison
William B. Harrison, Ohio
Charles M. Haskell, (Heiskell), Tenn.
Joseph M. Hawkins, Ireland

John M. Hays, Tenn.
Patrick Henry Herndon, Va.
William D. Hersee, England
Tapley Holland, Ohio
Samuel Holloway, Pa.
William D. Howell, Mass.
Thomas Jackson, Ireland
William Daniel Jackson, Ireland
Green B. Jameson, Ky.
Gordon C. Jennings, Conn.
Damacio Jimenes, Tex.
Lewis Johnson, Wales
William Johnson, Pa.
John Jones, N.Y.
Johnnie Kellog
James Kenney, Va.
Andrew Kent, Ky.
Joseph Kerr, La.
George C. Kimball, (Kimble), N.Y.
William P. King
William Irvine Lewis, Va.
William J. Lightfoot, Va.
Jonathan L. Lindley, IL.
William Linn, Mass.
Toribio Losoya, San Antonio
George Washington Main, Va.
William T. Malone, Va.
William Marshall, Tenn.
Albert Martin, Rhode Island
Edward McCafferty
Jesse McCoy, Tenn.
William McDowell, Pa.
James McGee, Ireland
John McGregor, Scotland
Robert McKinney, Ireland
Eliel Melton, Ga.
Thomas R. Miller, Tenn.
William Mills, Tenn.
Isaac Millsaps, Miss.
Edward F. Mitchusson, Va.
Edwin T. Mitchell
Napoleon B. Mitchell
Robert B. Moore, Va.
Willis Moore, Miss.
Robert Musselman, Ohio
Andres Nava, San Antonio
George Neggan, S.C.
Andrew M. Nelson, Tenn.
Edward Nelson, S.C.
George Nelson, S.C.
James Northcross, Va.
James Nowlan, Ireland
George Pagan, Miss.
Christopher Parker, Miss.
William Parks, N.C.

Richardson Perry
Amos Pollard, Mass.
John Purdy Reynolds, Pa.
Thomas H. Roberts
James Robertson, Tenn.
Isaac Robinson, Scotland
James M. Rose, Va.
Jackson J. Rusk, Ireland
Joseph Rutherford, Ky.
Isaac Ryan, La.
Mial Scurlock, N.C.
Marcus L. Sewell, England
Manson Shied, Ga.
Cleveland Kinlock Simmons, S.C.
Andrew H. Smith, Tenn.
Charles S. Smith, Md.
Joshua G. Smith, N.C.
William H. Smith
Richard Starr, England
James E. Stewart, England
Richard L. Stockton, Va.
A. Spain Summerlin, Tenn.
William E. Summers, Tenn.
William D. Sutherland, Ala.
Edward Taylor, Tenn.
George Taylor, Tenn.
James Taylor, Tenn.
William Taylor, Tenn.
B. Archer M. Thomas, Ky.
Henry Thomas, Germany
Jesse G. Thompson, Ark.
John W. Thomson, N.C.
John M. Thruston, Pa.
Burke Trammel, Ireland
William Barret Travis, S.C.
George W. Tumlinson, Mo.
James Tylee, N.Y.
Asa Walker, Tenn.
Jacob Walker, Tenn.
William B. Ward, Ireland
Henry Warnell, Ark.
Joseph G. Washington, Tenn.
Thomas Waters, England
William Wells, Ga.
Isaac White, Ky.
Robert White
Hiram J. Williamson, Pa.
William Wills
David L. Wilson, Scotland
John Wilson, Pa.
Anthony Wolfe, England
Claiborne Wright, N.C.
Charles Zanco, Denmark
John, Negro

James Bowie. Detail of a photograph from the Lucy Leigh Bowie Papers.
(The Daughters of the Republic of Texas Library. CN95.226)

William Barret Travis. Detail from a photograph of a painting by H. A. McArdle. DeShields Collection.
(The Daughters of the Republic of Texas Library. CN95.45)

Suggestions for Further Reading

Casteñeda, Carlos E., translator. *The Mexican Side of the Texas Revolution [1836]*. Dallas: P. L. Turner Company, 1928; Salem, New Hampshire: Ayer Company Publishers, Inc., 1976; New York: Arno Press, 1976.

De la Peña, José Enrique. *With Santa Anna in Texas: A Personal Narrative of the Revolution*. Translated and edited by Carmen Perry with an introduction by Llerena Friend. College Station: Texas A&M University Press, 1975.

Hardin, Stephen L. *Texian Illiad: A Military History of the Texas Revolution, 1835-1836*. Austin: University of Texas Press, 1994.

Lord, Walter. *A Time to Stand*. New York: Harper & Brothers, 1961; Lincoln and London: University of Nebraska Press, 1978.

Matovina, Timothy M. *The Alamo Remembered: Tejano Accounts and Perspectives*. Austin: University of Texas Press, 1995.

Tinkle, Lon. *13 Days to Glory: The Siege of the Alamo*. New York and other cities: McGraw-Hill Book Company, Inc., 1958; College Station: Texas A&M University Press, 1985.

Places to Visit

The Alamo. Alamo Plaza, San Antonio, Texas.

IMAX Theatre Rivercenter, 849 E. Commerce, San Antonio, Texas.